Why
so few
women
on the
street
at night

Sarona Abuaker

Published 2021 by the87press
The 87 Press LTD
87 Stonecot Hill
Sutton
Surrey
SM3 9HJ
www.the87press.co.uk

ISBN: 978-1-7399547-0-3

Design: Stanislava Stoilova [www.sdesign.graphics]

"We were circling around the thought of Chaos, sensing that the way Chaos itself goes around is the opposite of what is ordinarily understood by 'chaotic' and that it opens onto a new phenomenon: Relation, or totality in evolution, whose order is continually in flux and whose disorder one can imagine forever"

Édouard Glissant, *Poetics of Relation.*

"…we were planning to return. We left everything as it was"

Umm Yusif of Lifta, testimony recorded by Lena Jayyusi, *An Oral History of the Palestinian Nakba.*

For my parents and sereene.

Contents

Celluloid

apply to be recorded!
let me tell you what i cannot speak
the dysarthric underlings pulling below
afloat in bardo
sabulous swallowing
spit out azure light
in hopes we see our language carved in the sky

*

one Tuesday morning, i awoke to the world & discovered no
one* could see or hear We.

*

this is not a letter to a friend.
this is Victim Application 408 validly declared
----------is validity only declared by you or can i brandish this
declaration?
i declare this application legitimate filed under the case first
proceeded by Forensic Architecture – Emily Jacir
----------year 2019 / case name: zajal
[all proceeding images "Evidence" used in my file are from
their initial verbal correspondences between the architecture
firm & Jacir. See 'Letter to a Friend'
----------the Palestine ICC Proceedings. You may ask why i
did not file an application as a sub-clause with the already
existing preliminary approved chambers. The case just
doesn't really seem to grasp what i'm trying to get at – in fact
the case doesn't seem to grasp at anything at all.
----------anyhow before i get ahead of myself...}

i am filing Victim Application 408 on the behalf of said
victim
----------according to your definition i fit this category).
the crime against We is one of disappearance – for this i do
not know what i've done.
the disappearance follows, pursues me, holds me.

*

when a quantum observer is watching/particles can also
behave as waves. Electrons are "forced" to behave like
particles & not like waves whilst under observation. the act
of observation affects the experimental findings).

*

- faces Recording

?what is the distinction between archiving & surveillance?
3dir'beka dr'beka
the tear gas canister
"The Triple Chaser"
is the most fatal
because it breaks itself apart into three pieces to cover more
ground & bodies on its impact
3dir'beka dr'beka
the separating canister
according to the Defense Technologies website function
'Find a Dealer'
i can purchase tear gas from one of their suppliers within 40
miles of the city i used to live in

i can also experience it in the parts of Palestine i'm legally
only allowed to access in accordance with the "identity card"

issued to me

----------year 1999 (west bank permitted)

----------Jerusalem, 48' historical borders, the Gaza Strip are
non-permitted

Figure 1 | *Wearing "Evidence"*

see what we carry
the paper ink heaviness tongue cracked bones
are not just a bodily experience
they are policy
the red eyes stinging spluttering inhale (if you can)
rip the maps off our necks & carve into our chests
what you think is the most revolting thing about us
i don't just want a stamp in my "documents" "passport" "id card"
denying
entry
exit
curfew
water
family
friends
home

i want to feel the weight of your hatred on me
so i can measure the strength by which
i will need to muster
to hit you back

& you will feel it
in every way
towering over you
our voices filling the skies
our bodies shaking the streets
our hands on your "faces" "documents" "passports" "id cards"
"laws" "checkpoints" "surveillance" "towers" "guns"
ripping everything you have created
& making space making room
for the world We deserve to live in

six months later
We can be seen as a byproduct of two methodologies:

wearing "evidence"* relating to home of origin & showing
%erasure%

* "evidence" sprinkled onto pieces of transparent over-
head projector sheets act as material conduits between the
disappearing(s) skin & the external world. Images, graphs,
charts, statistics, maps, bank statements from the home of
origin &/or showing the said home of origins erasure embody
the forms of materiality the non-disappear require in order to
see the disappear(ings).

Figure 2 | *Initial Sketches of how to Wear "Evidence"*.

*theory tested a total of 54 times with various materials

[transparent over-head projector sheets opted over paper
due to weather temperaments. Ink from the required
materials – running down the face/body from unexpected
rain – is not a substitute]

The home of origin content is absolutely vital in creating
a barrier at which the non-disappeared/ing come to their
senses & open mouths/eyes (if able) to acknowledge. See
'Where Are You From'. See 'What Do You Think About
What is Happening There'.
(See 'Methods for Catapulting Oneself'

i walk into the local Budgens wearing Ghassan Kanafani's
Men in the Sun head to toe /chapter 1 starting at my
head & the story ending at my feet\ with no luck of being
sighted. The consequence is a stolen crème brûlée pot. For
this i am only partially sorry.

recommended usage:
side affects warning: processes of recognition[Da] *never started
or buffering for centuries*

[Da]: scientists have observed an odd strand of quantum
movement taking place in electrons moving among atomic
layers of a material. Rather than moving from bottom to top
layer [being observed to pass through the middle]
the electrons were seen to be disappearing
from the bottom layer and reappearing in the top layer
a fraction of a second later –

   with no trace of them existing in between.

*

i cannot tell you what it is like
starring at myself in the mirror
with someone standing next to me
who can only see themselves

*

skin organs tissue veins body
      building

        (3 stories: white grey green

        Story 1. green
        implodes rooted out of
        raised up torn from
        arms-branches
        restricting tears / water shortages
        a tree should not connotate shortened breath

        Story 2. grey
        thick dysthymiac toppings sludging
        thwack bang zrrrrrrrr wrrrrrrrrr bang bang
        our eulogies are sonic echoes
        made by their welcome mats
        {please tear out scabrous features}

Story 3. white

        10,611 dunams>

wearing*cruelty free vegan boots
they strap him to a chair
leather binding the top half of his body
lower half bound to the seat by rope
turn on the air conditioner
leave
(windows door wide open
            - a night in December

        where do you go when i give up all of my cards?
"checkmate"
"ace"
"full-house"
do you slam your hands on the table & yell
"it's a bingo!"
or curl into yourself a snail looking for the shell that once
harbored the body
soft safe warm
away
        or does it make you want to grab a gun
----------buy a gun!
t-shirts generate bumptious flailing
i walk in the park (hilly fields)
i see two people
walking towards my direction smiling i smile back
(a southern flaw)
to realize their eyes on my chest
starring
their smiles not really smiles
more like

boxed mouths
gritting
plastered emerging when one
eats something they find to be foul
but is too repressed /british\
to spat it out
i look down
i see the outline of a place with a name
on it
We are the shit you cannot spit out.

*

you want a diaphanous tongue
blow on the ear
goosebumps on the arm/neck
obeisance until the touch becomes a graze
until the camera turns back on you
until you are the one who cannot leave the hold

*

i hope this is enough
----------i don't care if it isn't].

*

Figure 3 | *Wearing "Evidence"* #2

scarify; indrench; indurate/
faqqua iris covered surveillance towers
do not block a sniper's aim.

*

smiling
awash in exhilaration at the fate of being
eaten by us sweet
whipped cream piped
teddy bear cake
arms outstretched towards the betunia night sky
We only had to pass
through two checkpoints to be here
        i will not tell you
the family and friends who risked
"Residencies"
"Jobs"
"15,000 shekel fines"
to cross with us
to see the sea

*

release memory
        muscle
heart
if you cut open the chest
you will see the blockages
cross lines
coronary
green azygous
armistice
partition
seizing seizing seizing

Figure 4 | *Wearing "Evidence" #3*

*

exulting ------
---------- despair
pay $100 scanning
effervesce hiding away
tucked behind ear
swallow keep tight in throat
solid fatiscente grounds
she holds an ipad
when she asks me to select the dates i was in the west bank
she compliments the henna blooming my hands
dotting fingers / a farewell in flesh
before i can stop myself
a thank you crumples out of my mouth
a funambulist
upon passing i spit my name on the concrete

*

interrogated for eight hours
20 times they asked "why are you here? why do you want
to return?"

*

i'm not exactly sure why this is being sent to you.
i suppose it seems the proper thing to do
– an application to tell you of my present disappearance,
so that it can be recorded even if i will not
be recognized as disappearing [or at all

]

you are institutionally positioned, contractually obligated
to read this.

----------but what good does that do?
this is not an application to appearance.
i do not want to be summoned back into the world
where disappearance pervades.
this has ceased to be an application.
it has become something else entirely.
you are the one not able to step away.
even after ceasing your activity of reading this
you will remain here.
We know what it is
to feel the flame engulfed in the gaze of another
We wear "evidence"
----------for now
the day will come when We take it off
leaving it on the ground
some of We are laying these certain images down
for something else altogether
what does that mean for you?
where does this leave you?
the all-consuming eyes hanging open mouth
slack dribbling seething ravenous
perhaps you're not hungry at all
insulin dripping into you is all We are
keeping you in floating bureaucratic linearity

Figure 4 | *Wearing "Evidence" #3*

How to start a fire in the wild with nothing

we are no longer eligible to be exploited by a certain entity
it's the ring in your ear after an explosion –
air fighter jets over my flat
friction based living –
hand drill in frontal cortexes
i'm told to re-train to acquire a different job

i say to them:

> i am comfortable telling people what they need to do
> i will get involved if i think i can help
> i make decisions quickly
> i am good at coming to an agreement with other people
> i like to take control of situations
> i like working with numbers
> i enjoy getting involved in practical task
> i prefer to follow what other people are doing
> i like taking responsibility for other people
> i like to follow rules and processes
> i am comfortable talking in front of a group of people
> i think i am a competitive person
> i set myself goals in life
> i enjoy planning a task more than actually doing it
> i am comfortable talking people around to my way of
>   thinking
> i like meeting new people
> i find it hard to understand other people's point of view
> i like to help other people
> i enjoy working with other people around me
> i want to make things better for people doing well in a
> career motivates me

i am comfortable hearing other people's problems
i like to work out complicated things
i like working with facts
i like to get to the centre of the issue
i like to see the results of the work i do
i enjoy learning new things
i enjoy coming up with new ways of doing things
i try to think differently to others
i like to use my imagination to create new things
i like to focus on details
i plan my day so i can use my time best
i like to try new things
i feel restricted when i have to follow a routine
i like doing things in a careful order
i enjoy creative activities
i set myself targets when i have things to do
i like working with my hands or tools
i like to see things through to the end

what they say when they colonize us

Administration
agreement
unofficial
survey
official
war
establish
recognition
state-building
negotiations
illegitimate
sovereign
partition
mandate
civil
development
encouragement
co-operation
entrusted
peace
initiative
investors
guidelines
self-interim
stipulations
coexistence
mutual
international supervision
public order
joint committee
coordination

incentives
profit
opportunities
market allocation
positive sanctions
polities
aid

My Mother's Third Imprisonment

Conceive this moment
come to understand it(')s history

soldiers shove a tray of olives
        under the door
she carves
        holes into the pits
                using a nail finds
                        a string
                                makes a bracelet.
resistance sometimes looks like constraint.
her cell lined with used tea bags
                                strung up drying
waiting for reuse throughout the weeks.

the soldiers do not come around.

The Hours

[4.00am]

In case you don't find what you seek

look in
 trash cans
  coat pockets linings
   trouser pockets
   jewelry boxes
    his favorite critical theory books
     ambiguous novels
      South African pottery
      bloodied tissues
       in between the pages of unwrapped printer paper
       CD lyric booklets

        empty brown delivery boxes
        DVD covers
         under the bed
          behind the bed
           underneath the Persian rugs
           bathroom breaks
           recent calls

             text messages
              accidental screenshots
               private numbers
                eyes flickering
                 widening dilated
                  pupils pinpointing to

[10.36am]

i want to sleep
without dreaming
of you
fucking other women

[5.30pm]

light the wick
throw it at the enemy
choke on gasoline
it comes from my insides
out spitting

[9.25pm]

survey the landscape
there
do you see
where is it?
the queen orders for a Jaffa box
she bites
her teeth crack
on the seeds

i'm fucking tired

Remove my organs
as a block
start at my neck
follow the vagus
crack my ribs
make an omelette
autopsy for clarification –

Yes i want you to grovel

Put in take out. stock stock stock. add stock. not too salty; so it takes you out from the house/takes your house; just enough to keep getting on by manipulating the system is not necessarily challenging it – it's just using it differently. i want to see wall street bankers on the streets and their domestic workers living in their mansions. i want to see wall street bankers beg for food and be thrown a penny. i want to see wall street bankers walk into a subway foot infected a foul smell emitting from. wall street bankers are the rot, the stench, the infection, the cancer spreading in every part of your body when you just went to the doctor for a cough. before they took our house i wrote lines from capital on the walls inside cupboards on the doors. i didn't want whoever occupied the space to have a pleasant experience. i did this while we sold our fridge, bedroom sets, chairs, couches to people who've known us for years but they didn't look at us the same. instead with wide round eyes pity cramming every corner sinking the eyelids down so heavy they just starred at the floor. uneasy embarrassed that we could no longer hide behind loans, borrowing money taking out capital in another name. [No, honey just because i have a laptop does not mean i am middle class]. so they took the house we lived in for 12 years because we could not afford to keep making payments. where were you in 2008 harboring yourself behind gold doors. yes i want to see you outside on the streets with nowhere to go yes i want to see you telling your family you cannot afford to rent a room. yes i want to see you live through what millions of others have had to go through because of you because of your greed. this shock you are experiencing is because you thought you were safe, untouchable, protected. this is your sign, your letter, your fate, notifying you that you are indeed within arm's reach.

Lithospheric Motions

Today sadness is a river and i am in it
                    swimming-moving-through
                        it for
this is what i'm learning
to do
not-sink.   When i find myself waking up
                    understanding how to embrace
                            the water lays itself inside me
                            fills itself deep in valleys known as
                            deep depressions
                            deep formations

  cracking   open
                    the earth for us to peer inside
they normally hold water
and to be able to hold all that water
                    for us to be able to see the valley and water for
what   it is
        you have to understand how it got there
                                        how it came to-be
thousands of years   eroding   rain   sun   wind   slapping
heating
tugging at this earth for so long.

what lines the explosions

waterfalls drop in our chests
vagus climbs [the head opens]
skull breaks in pieces
      brain slicks & bumps
        look i say
          pointing to my cranium
            blood spurts
              onto fingers
                falls to the ground
              this is the motherboard
            when i look into your eyes
           my frontal cortex shivers with pleasure
          it soothes my autonomic nervous system
          when i hear your voice
          i want to scream
            in simultaneous pain and delight
            ----what to do?
            hexagons
            pentagons
        squares
      no matter how many
      sides-shapes & puzzles i try
      i circle to the end-start

Suture Fragmentations – a note on return

"To stand with us in this circle with its centre everywhere and its circumference now/here is to be under a spell. A pleasure to meet you here: enchanted"[1]

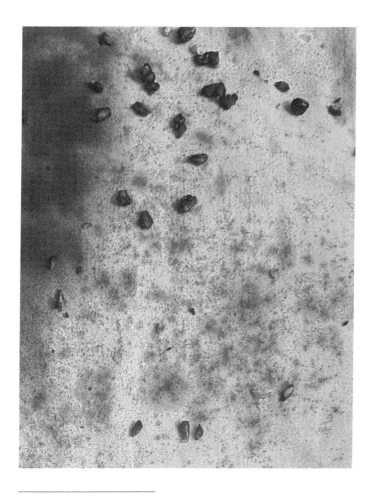

[1]Shin, Sarah & Tamás, Rebecca. 2018. Spells: 21st – Century Occult Poetry. Ignota.

Shortly after finishing an essay exploring how Palestinian's abilities to produce aesthetics inherently carves new spaces to resist Israeli settler colonialism, i visited Basma Alsharif's exhibition *The Gap Between Us* at the Mosaic Rooms in London.[2] It was Alsharif's first independent UK exhibition, comprised of three pieces originating from different moments in her practice. Overlaying a multiplicity of images and sounds from original film footage taken from different locations she visited, Alsharif stitches together rich tapestries of reimagined spaces and times as an intimate navigation through her ideas of what Palestinian imagination and memory re/building can look like as a Palestinian in diaspora. Filming in France, Italy, California, the Gaza Strip, Malta and Athens, she weaves aesthetics familiar to the Palestinian national struggle amongst a backdrop of unfamiliar landscapes, and interrogates the elasticity of what is constituted as familiar Palestinian cultural forms by challenging the audience and herself with the question, "what do you do when civilization has failed you? What happens if the Right of Return is never granted – what will this mean for Palestinians?"[3]

[2]Alsharif, B. (2018). *The Gap Between Us*. [Film Footage] London: The Mosaic Rooms.

[3]Basma Alsharif by Aily Nash. (2015). BOMB. [online] Available at: https://bombmagazine.org/articles/basma-alsharif/.

"*To be orientated around something is not so much to take up that thing, as to be taken up by something, such that one might even become what it is that is 'around'*"

Ahmed, S. 2006. Queer Phenomenology. Duke University Press Books.

Moving from piece to piece, Alsharif's unflinching questions on return, memory re/building and futuristic aesthetic reconfigurations have followed and not left me since. Emerging from the collision of her cultural forms constituting as Palestinian expressions was not only a reshaped understanding of resistance, but a shift in how to engage with and produce Palestine and Palestinian's relationship with diaspora. The conditions involved in experiencing displacement, nation-state building, and identity formation are not unique to Palestinians or to the Palestinian national struggle. These themes, however, have become synonymous to Palestinian ontology due to their repetition and juxtaposition within Palestinian cultural production as strategic methods to evoke indigenous claims in the face of ongoing Israeli settler colonialism.

Necessitating the physical and cultural erasure of the indigenous, settler colonialism "comes with the intention of making a new home on the land, a homemaking that insists on settler sovereignty over all things in their new domain"[4]. The reality of dispossession impacts Palestinians' ways of engaging, moving in, and experiencing Palestine on the physical realm of being able to access the land. Out of this physical uprooting, and the response to it, is a production of Palestinian-ness tied to a "place-bound definition (which) focuses on return, and home is defined as from where one came"[5]. Returning to Palestine functions as not only the point of origin for how Palestinians come to identify themselves, but as an activator for aesthetic production as

---

[4]Tuck, E. and Yang, K. (2012). Decolonization Is Not A Metaphor. Decolonization: Indigeneity, Education & Society, [online] 1(1), pp.1-40. Available at: https://jps.library.utoronto.ca/

[5]Peteet, J. (2007). PROBLEMATIZING A PALESTINIAN DIASPORA. International Journal of Middle East Studies, 39(04), pp.1-21.

it reflects conditions of exile. Expressions of return in all its dimensions have become the prevailing cultural discourse for engagement with Palestine and Palestinian-ness, especially for Palestinians in diaspora. When Palestinians' common capacity to engage with themselves exists mainly through this framework, how does this shape Palestinian diasporic ontologies? What happens when this concept of return is no longer the exclusive departure point?

*

return

"to come back or
go back to a place or
 person/architecturally –
continue (a wall) in a changed
direction, especially at
                              right angles"[6]

the notion of return, or returning, glimmers
           r i p p l i n g m o v e m e n t s.

this is a poem colonizers'
           will
           cut
           their hands on
chronic wounds
                    splintering

---

[6] "Definition Of RETURN". 2020. Merriam-Webster.Com.
https://www.merriam-webster.com/dictionary/return.

return is inherently an experiment in phenomenology;
to go or come back is a beckoning of how to arrive.
Alsharif's gaps directs the viewer to stitched spatialities and
temporalities in order to interrogate return. It is here, in this
moment of being re-turned to experience a return by her
films i found what was relegated to the background of my
life but i was always----x

x------ arriving to -------x
palestinian-ness as a queer dimension and the possibilities of
queering return---x

*

arriving
involves questions
timing, space, direction.
can we arrive, recognize we are arriving
if it is not thought out? It is a question of being in
a certain order – one that defies settler-colonial ordering.
to arrive to a place not on the map means thinking beyond what we see
pushing my body and vision in different, multiple ways to create new
shapes, forms of thought.

We keep moving
i hear her say
he didn't roll down his window
fast enough to

throw the Molotov.
                    Re/(O)pen

he walks from Lebanon to Syria
taking off his socks
                he finds
                        his skin comes off.

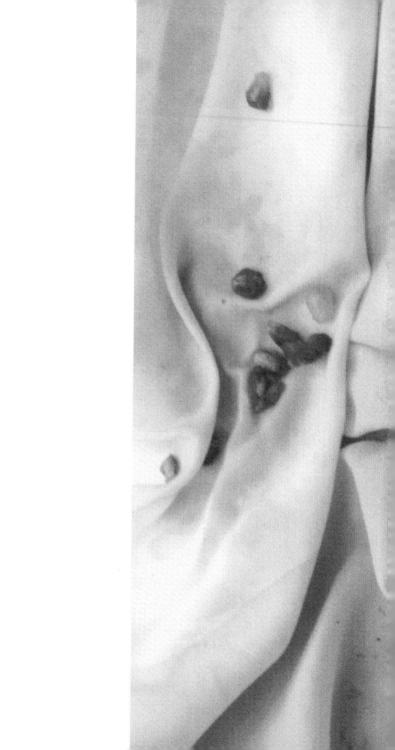

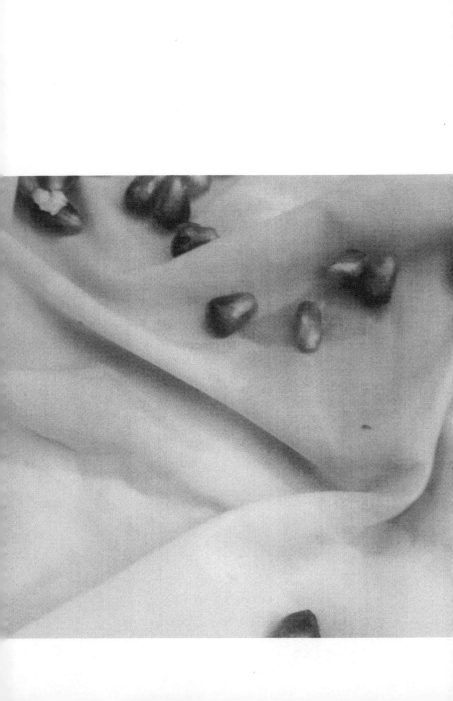

"Becoming reoriented
which involves the disorientation of encountering
the world differently, made me wonder about orientation
and how much 'feeling at home'
or knowing which way we are facing
is about the making of worlds"

Ahmed, S. 2006. Queer Phenomenology. Duke University Press Books.

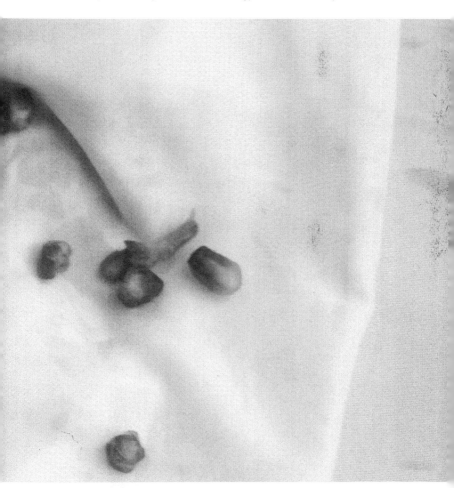

Alsharif's pieces spoke to a queerness already present; i was able to recognize the beats, rhythms, sutured landscapes, and disorientations for they mirrored, resonated with my own. Queerness of/being out of place in (diaspora), whilst pointing to queerness in Palestinian-ness. Her films made me think of how my experience of inheriting a homeland with a certain direction towards it, with a certain nature of relationality; to be Palestinian in many ways is to be constituted as an "unnatural"[7]occurrence for it pushes back against a hegemonic narrative reproducing Israel's settler-colonial epistemologies.

Without our ancestor's
masks (what are they?)

To be "off the map" is to embody uncharted territory, alien, not realized, not true. With lines on maps and countries carved as though they are as natural tectonic plate shifts, Palestinian-ness has been affixed in a certain direction, rooted in a certain force due to ongoing erasure and seeking a return.

We don't scatter   we are
elastic   stretching
                                     beyond

their wildest dreams

Queerness here means the processes and acts of re-orienting

---

[7]Seymour, Nicole. 2013. Strange Natures: Futurity, Empathy, And The Queer Ecological Imagination.

return in relation to times, spaces, us. Return has always then, been conceived as "unnatural" for it is a practice of making an order beyond the state-sanctioned order which we live today, a "capitalist domestication"[8] and settler-colonial regimes. i propose return as practice; queering return so it re-aligns with orientations of possibility, a way of directing through future-thinking. Return as spatial occurrences.

[8] Seymour, Nicole. 2013. Strange Natures: Futurity, Empathy, And The Queer Ecological Imagination.

How does queer phenomenology help us think about living return in different spaces and being re-turned in spaces? It is an inching 'towards', and i want to think about what moving a towards and where that towards may be, to retexturize the feel of life

> we shape ourselves
> with the force
> of each other
> carve new spaces and times
> wringing out
> sea water

i am moved to queer return as a possibility of occurring and being encountered in many places for i am moved by it in a multiplicity of spaces, times, touches, gestures and articulations. This piece is an attempt to start re-directing, gathering my bearings and senses, only to return to them back to you as a reader and see what takes shape in this exchange. Creating new forms means moving, taking other directions and making new movements. There are specificities to how return gathers itself around me, and my intention is to highlight who is able to face return. There are tensions in the particularities of facing return one way for it is not one dimension or position. This is also an experiment in relationalities.

i am arriving in return/its multiplicity of dimensions.

*

Return(ing) is acknowledging and grappling absences; the familiar conditions which have been producing effects on Palestinians take shape by becoming unnoticed in their iterabilities. Understandings of return are mainly produced by perceptions, touch, articulations, and movements embodying reaching for a location. i use queer phenomenology in attempt to re-turn us around return to show the queerness of this endeavor, to show the queerness of Palestinian-ness; to show how the shapes of returns are generated by how we are coming to be and the conditions of arrivals. By facing return as only one-way, perhaps i am erasing other ways of looking at return; perhaps bringing forth return to show how it exists in a multiplicity of spaces and not defined/constrained to a perception shaped by the very system which blocks a particular arrival can be an exercise of shedding light on the nearness of return(ing). It is a way of world-making through new movements and senses. i want to change the feeling of return by re(turn)ing the possibilities of where return arrives, can be found, and can be touched.

*

Categorizing strictly through the nation-state has become an atmospheric experience developing and shaping our senses of the world for it lends itself as an inherent departure point for how people imagine themselves and has become the only legitimate way of conceptualizing oneself. Legitimate here means the way in which hegemonic structural systems come to envelope one's aura through their recognizability of nation-ness and belonging to a state. Being Palestinian in many ways is queer due to the multiple dimensions i occupy – past, present, future, to not be recognized by states, inheriting a homeland without being in it. i am embodying an encapsulation of times, spaces, legacies and fragments. These fragmentations are a result of the establishment of Israel in 1948 "resulting in the devastation of Palestinian society. At least 80 percent of the Palestinians who lived in the major part of Palestine upon which Israel was established – more than 77 percent of Palestine's territory – became refugees"[9]. The Nakba, catastrophe, simultaneously induced an uprooting in common Palestinian senses and expression. It is for this reason that i use fragmentation as a form for writing this piece.

the children
of those who were expelled
were colors.
Each one imbued
turning to each other and say
what if we were there
at the same time
together

Settler-colonialism ruptures the forms of times and spaces cultivated by the indigenous to the land; these times and spaces splinter and become carried in different ways, from oral narrativization to cultural production. The time and spaces which were violently uprooted change in forms, textures, gestures, tongue, memory and touch – it is experiencing shock and disorientation on every level.

*

The creation and maintenance of Israel relies on the erasure of sensory experiences and understandings constituting Palestinian-ness. Erasure of sensory experiences, being able to locate oneself   occurs

      on

   multiple

        levels.

---

[9]Abu-Lughod, L. and Sa'di, A. (2007). Nakba: Palestine, 1948, and the Claims of Memory (Cultures of History). New York: Columbia University Press, pp.1-24.

(sometimes dehiscent
i |close| the stitches
find them re/(o)pened
tissue replaces
dermis as epidermis in motion
biochemical immunity)

*

Settler-colonial erasure involves the unbinding of lines drawn around and, on the surfaces, which come to be felt as fact and knowledge; a violent systematic deliberate targeting to unravel what gives form to our lives. From re-drawing lines on a map, constituting written, textual forms as more 'valid' than oral forms narrativizing experiences, freezing Palestinian bank accounts, stealing literature, films, and images, to home demolitions and expulsions. Israeli settler-colonialism, like other examples of settler-colonialism, embodies how colonial state-building practices relies on the literal and aesthetic re-orientating of the indigenous.

Taking the 'desert to make it bloom', a common trope emerging from Israeli settler colonial Soviet style posters[10], showing from a birds-eye-view a lush valley sunken by the weight of happy, well-fed and cultivated trees meant to be representing Jaffa. Each tree bright, carrying engorged ripe sun-blasted oranges with a hand reaching towards the orange, a hand outstretched ready and eager to pick the fruity gem the land produced, for the land is grateful that a civilizing force has swept over it. The force is often embodied through the figure represented as a woman, smiling coyly as she picks the oranges for it is not only produce she is gathering, she is

---

[10]Sivan, Eyal. 2009. Jaffa, The Orange's Clockwork. Video.

also producing lines of power and being received in certain directions solidifying the making of Israel.

As said woman picks oranges, lines appear into the land where homes once were - - - - straightening lines, where the native homes embodying the 'perversion', the 'queerness', the 'odd' ways in which the native inhabits the space. The being of Palestinian-ness in a space transformed into a threat to the state-building order; to be Palestinian embodied a direction of not just 'backwards' but of being bent towards an idea, a physical discomfort for the new state because it was and continues to be a body that takes up space and in taking up space produces a shape which is not desired.

"The contemporary history of the Palestinians turns on a key date: 1948. That year, a country and its people disappeared from maps and dictionaries... "The Palestinian people does not exist," said the new masters, and henceforth the Palestinians would be referred to by general, conveniently vague terms, as either "refugees," or in the case of a small minority that had managed to escape the generalized expulsion, "Israeli Arabs." A long absence was beginning"[11]

[11]Abu-Lughod, L. and Sa'di, A. (2007). Nakba: Palestine, 1948, and the Claims of Memory (Cultures of History). New York: Columbia University Press, pp.1-24.

Palestinian-ness became a being that was outside of the state logic. And as this line of thinking follows, we emanate a queerness for "when bodies 'arrive' that don't extend the lines already extended by spaces, then those spaces might even appear 'slantwise' or 'oblique'[12].

The length of time maintaining expulsions, and how dominance is re-asserted through the settler-colonial apparatus, whether here or there, accumulate and matter. Forms of dominance by Israel are expressed through the ability to create distances. Return is mainly approached as a thing which must appear only because it is perceived as a moment that has been blocked from its entry. Distance is not only a physical separation. Distances are not composed of matters which end when the separation ends, or when a recognized form of arrival arrives. It takes work to illuminate and thrive amidst gaps and spaces – but what about the matters at hand which we re-turn to do the work of return(ing) towards these openings and fragments? If return(ing) will take on the shapes of the conditioning from our bodies, who will be the ones who shape our pasts/presents/futures? The Nakba did not end, it only continues to devastate in re-fashioned ways.

---

[12]Ahmed, Sara. 2006. Queer Phenomenology. Duke University Press Books

It is here i intervene in a form of return. i want to turn now to look at the matter return can be/is made of. This attempt of thinking through return is an invitation to think about what matters about ourselves. The stuff of situating, measuring, arriving, leaving to and in around/ourselves.

Return is an embodiment of labour and work – who is taking it upon themselves to ensure return emerging? Writing this piece is a form of labour. i am suggesting return(ing) can be/ is composed of such matters, such labours at hand. There is a question of the value of looking at how these navigations matter at all, especially to return(s). The value of tensions, unfurling them, matter for behavior matters. Return(ing) is not a matter at hand that should be brushed off, taken into others hands who will bring forth return(ing) as a commodity, which presented by hegemonic powers "is changed into something transcendent"[13].

Walking through Ramallah in Spring 2019 underneath construction and buildings, increasing in height by the year, positioning visions of Prada and Dolce & Gabbana conveniently located underneath luxury flats. Futures front and center to pedestrians whilst the leadership keeps billboards than the people or streets themselves. These are affects brought forth from the non-queerness of this world.

Couture shops able to exist more easily than the very people who've been here for centuries.
   A disorienting touch, senses of fugitivity. i am gripped (in wanting) to not be right
    side up
if this vision is what is meant to be
the linear perceptible path.

---

[13] Ahmed, Sara. 2006. Queer Phenomenology. Duke University Press Books.

*

Neoliberal imaginations taking up space, the affects of histories co-opted for state-building as a practice for a return exclusively enjoyed by banks, private investors, newly gated community owners. A commodification of practices shape the form of return – is 'it' still return if the very motions that kicked my mother, sister and i out of our home in the states take space in Palestine under a different flag?

Return(ing) is not about trying to find forgiveness/refuge from debt in one boundary only to accumulate it in another. Return(ing) is not about showing solidarity for blackness in one place/language only to arrive to another and allow those very poisoning anti-black articulations/gestures to proliferate in a different tongue.

Return is not something separate from our contact with others; it is a shape made by our relationalities.

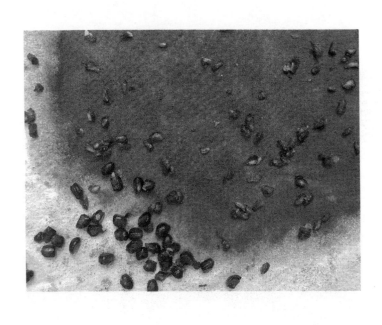

Where am i? Why is this here? What is here and what needs to be in its place? It is a "queer disorientation, the absence of coherence, but not of things, in the moving presence of absolutely nothing"[14].

It is a hold unlike any other.
                    Soldiers fire tear gas
              i ran holding myself to the sea
washing away the agent only to find our photographs drowned.

[14]Harney, Stefano, and Moten, Fred. 2013. The Undercommons: Fugitive Planning & Black Study. Wivenhoe: Minor Compositions.

Understandings of return often arrive at forms of touch/i have a dimension of return for it is a right/which i am enshrined with by having UN Resolution 194.

"The United Nations General Assembly adopts resolution 194 (III), resolving that "refugees wishing to return to their homes and live at peace with their neighbours should be permitted to do so at the earliest practicable date, and that compensation should be paid for the property of those choosing not to return and for loss of or damage to property which, under principles of international law or equity, should be made good by the Governments or authorities responsible."[15]

As the UN General Assembly described in the above paragraph in 1948, the emergence of return in this proscribed space and time relies on certain positionalities, certain directions to be taken place. Return must be 'practicable', the qualities of this practicable return must be made 'good' (for whom?) or compensated (by whose measure?) by the 'Governments or authorities responsible' (when has this ever happened?).

Under whose return is this practicable? Nonetheless, 'refugees' is left completely unformed – one dimensional. Static. Return emerges as a stack of bones in the corner. Swept aside. Out of sight out of mind. Where is return in any 'peace process' resolution, other than the nuisance it presents itself to be – the insect on the ground of your kitchen floor scuttling away with the corner of your favorite independence day cake in its mouth.

---

[15]UN General Assembly 194 UNRWA
https://www.unrwa.org/content/resolution-194

What position does this interpretation, this practice, this linear, straight state suit making return leave us in? This isn't to dismiss the dire necessity of this dimension of return needing to happen; a physical return especially for those who are experiencing forms limbo for the last several decades. i know all too well the number of spaces my blue U.S.A. passport allows me to breezily walk into – entering the United Kingdom where i currently reside the borders become more insidiously porous through technological aesthetic data harvesting methods. No more do i oftentimes need a person to ask me where i was – i hold a document enshrined with a status which allows me to head straight to machines where i swipe it. Doors open and i walk into a different country. Buying fruits at the self-checkout in Sainsbury's can often feel more like a tedious task than the border. This does not mean i am not direct line of violence – it means the line i am "walking into in that moment, in that space, is extended to me in this particular dimension"[16].

[16]Ahmed, Sara. 2006. Queer Phenomenology. Duke University Press Books.

Are these the forces we leave to shape return? Britain after all has a role in this mess.

i am set in a different direction quite literally from others who hold other documents from other places. And the state sanctifies itself to hold these people differently

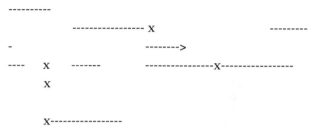

The line designed to walk within is quite literally straight whereas people who hold 'other' documents require more spaces –
     to wait

         to stand

               more cubicles to
show the line is not to be followed without a break but to expect breaks

to expect deviations for you/your (body) becomes the deviation. You become questioned, you become the question in of itself which must be answered – the first curiosity always aligning with that of spatiality

"where have you come from?"

In many ways i hold two molecular embodiments – benefiting from being born in a space which institutionally rejects my very embodiment if i were to be born in the city where my mother was born.

(if someone is denied access to Jerusalem for
over 40 years because they are constituted
as a threat based solely on their nationality,
denied a return, to then be granted a visa
after reaching the age of 50 for the state
no longer considers this numerological
arrival a threat – is this deviance restored
to a rightful state order? Their being, one
day being constituted as a perversion to the
state's ethno-sanctity, now being granted
permission to be in these certain spatiality
– new lines open, new orientations are
available, but the texture is still that of the
states, of the settler-colonial ordering.)

"And so it is we remain in the hold, in the break, as if
entering again and again the broken world, to trace the
visionary company and join it"[17].

We deviate in our world-making. i remain in this hold –
crashing and crashing into this world, shattering and re-
shattering to see the fragments and find ways of making new
worlds in these profound and heart-wrenching futurisms.
'Tracing' as Moten and Stefanno say, the line of deviations,
return to spaces we've been to only to find ourselves re-
turned. Orientating to others in these visionary lines. i take
certain directions to make certain returns – to make those
returns/desires seem possible. i align with other's lines if their
return(ings) is a matter of being.

Being in return, being returned, be-coming return. It is 'the

[17]Harney, Stefano, and Moten, Fred. 2013. The Undercommons: Fugitive
Planning & Black Study. Wivenhoe: Minor Compositions.

refugee' who needs to be 'returned' – a certain position, a deviation from state-making order. Taking it upon ourselves of doing the work to ensure return does not become a commodity.

To own what i am made of/making and what i aim to be, to push forward return as not a single act dictated by hegemonic states, but as pieces of practices encompassing every dimension of life means return is an emancipation of the senses; i push return forward not as a policy which must wait until a linear achievement of Palestinian sovereignty becomes a land form. It is not the end point – it is an ongoing departure. Queering return by re-positioning it as not only a physical dimension of physically returning to Palestine if that is what is chosen by Palestinians, but also occupying multiple times and spaces of practice for Palestinian-ness occupies those very things. i am queering return by facing it as a Palestinian born and raised outside of Palestine – there is a plurality of things within Palestinian-ness which are relegated to the background by hegemonic powers; the starkest example is recognizability of Palestine/Palestinians, including return and also the role of diaspora in world-making.

Fugitivity
is
a rhythm
soft
in the under
salve palliates
the proliferations
we do not need to be
assuaged
we need to set fire

x-----   ----- x

New Stories We Tell Ourselves

extraction a drawing out
peel each word back
disentangle all
the parts
lay them out on a table
examine the curves
sharp edges
lines of each letter
see what else we can bring forth from what we see.

Debt

set up a trap for debt
collectors
welcome them to come to
your front door
drop a safe on their heads
so they can feel the weight of
what you are overdue

Walking on Portobello Road/
Laa sha3ra ras al 3mood

The top of the hill asks why
there are so few women on the streets
at night they split   so wide now
so open   swallowing bullets whole
i step off the tube into a service
reaching for an oyster pulling out a blue shekel rolling into
itself foaming at the mouth a tasree7 flashes gold
my necklace stops me gun and finger in face he looks at my
chest and says "sarona"
          heart hammer
          smith and city line leaving - is that your name?

Why is your name   Arab

Where did you come   From

Why are you   Here

– checking points to checkpoint –
no curfews from Brockley to Al Sharafe
they only put padlocks on our homes when the banks take them
she screams they are coming on fire
storming city buildings demanding
answers for the dead cannot move but they speak
through what we create
his face painted into city steel cranes towering skies eyes
black graffitied sunken deep into the walls beneath watching
their shadows
                              torturing uniforms

our cacti can still be found   we water
ourselves in memories and imagination

thorns prickling stabbing

                              there are some things

                              refusing to be touched.
My hands trace over the white jutting stone
three stories tall
each story for a family   each story is empty and
still with silence

                    in such spaces where we are walking
on our graves
she picked up her friends' brains s p l a t t e r e d on the sidewalk
she put rose water on them afterwards
summoning smoothness from the hardness
        Plunging into the sea
a Blue and White *Bon Voyage*! before entering Jericho from
Shepherds Bush
soldiers telling my mother to leave her one-year old daughter
at the border so she can move on.
We must struggle to imagine what love will look like in
liberation.

Laa sh3ra ras al 3mood – No, *the street at the head of the
hill (a street in Jerusalem)*
Tasree7 – visa

(being kept alive by a ticking time bomb)

Rough powder
terrain
it's when you close your eyes
moving in a vehicle
you can feel the sun padding your eyelids
the light changes
follows on top of you

its like that

warning signs
                    diaphragm
                        ex
                    -panding
                    closing in
              watching a person
              intently focusing
                    on speed
                  speech roar
              in a crowd buzzing
                  squawking
                              (did someone see these
poor attempts)

i've never read on the sensations of
        – but have felt
someone else's lifeline synced to mine

detonations
        peel face
                back

skin falls apart in shreds
only the eyes remain
        still watching
            him.
                    (what do you do when a place
                            is under bombardment?)
            – return.
            – keep returning
stumble chocked

flesh stretched thin
pulled down to earth
        to the inside of
a black hole orbits

strong hold

        heart lungs ribs

                                in left hand
        stomach intestines
                in right
                        i run to you
                                back
            return

each time
        i find you
                splattered

                        face bloated
                        caved in
                            (i don't recognize this)
on the pavement

                        maggots feast on the hands
                        i held

                                        twitch as they
make their way down into
                    tendons flexors abductors
                                        (i come to expect you
                                        hope each time
                                        to see something else)

i brace myself
for each return
                            join you
                                    in the descent
                            – nervous systems nervous
                                    each time something else is lost

until one day
                you are not on the ground
                        but standing up
                                detonator removed
                                        and on the ground.

i have been trying to leave the pavement since.

Work

Abash surplus snatchers
language adumbratively
sets me on fire

the boss
strikes a
match
against
my forehead
it lights
aflame
burning
my eyelashes
the boss
distances
the match
feigning
adynamia
as if the
conditions
created to
enable the
match to
be formed
from a tree
lighted
tossed
was not from
their own hands

Harmonious conflagrations

thwack thwack smack
thwack thwack thud
wrrr wrrr wrrr –
spinning right

hands interlaced
palms pressed flat
against each other
bound
a whirring unanimous

each part playing a part
thud thud thud crash!
meeting in the centre
thwack thwack thack
thudding spinning
smacking feet on the ground
stomping up
again and again
to you we reach

synchronicity

"my dear, don't be afraid, it's nothing, it will pass"

Incessant tongues pluck the mouth
cast iron skillets burn
dowsing yourself in milk won't do
gulping gallons won't take out the flame
soothe blisters
bubbles in trachea
– your people are acting like assholes though you have to admit
i turn away from the face
 it's a party turned diplomatic conference
 everyone is appointed UN General Secretaries
 a private imitation of a public
put on trial eating veggie hotdogs
inhale and choke on Jenny McCartney
dispersion is a separation; a distribution it informs a
movement of scattering from one center to a wide area
the center will not only hold it grows
not imitation that is for
the settlers
parroting perfecting the art of squawking
 flying nest the cuckoo
who carries machine guns in the street
smashes its cars into pedestrians
drags Palestinians from their homes
bombs white phosphorous onto children's
schools
burns olive tree
valleys
chains trees to buildings
they may stomp their feet on the earth
(it spits them back out regurgitating poison)
a colonial masquerading

'heros of the text and failures of thought'[18]
 the text is meant to imitate something they don't believe
was ever in existence
a ghost a specter
is their blueprint A -> B
                    we give flesh to the void in their imaginations
we become the unimaginable walking running stomping
fucking eating celebrating writing breathing we want to do all
on our land
let's meet in

       [stun – the flash momentarily triggers all cells in
       the eye that respond to light, blinding it for about
       five seconds, forcing it to see an afterimage that
       threatens vision. The amount of volume induced by
       the detonation also creates temporary deafness and
       unsettles fluid in the ear, bringing about a loss of
       balance]

parading around pompous seals slapping their fins on the
rocks dive headfirst into the dead sea
very material playing house with a guillotine, they were the
kids who dismember their barbies in the name of medical
examination
arrest 500 there's 7 million more not within
your reach
flatten the strip there's hands
ready to rebuild
if you don't take it someone
will

---

[18] Gordon, Lewis R. What Fanon Said.

if you don't take it someone else
----doesn't have to

Newton's first law of

motion

"An object at
rest stays at
rest
and an object in   motion

stays   in
motion

with the same
speed
and in the same direction
unless acted upon by
an unbalanced force."

Objects
"keep on
doing what
they're
doing."

Objects

tend to resist changes
in their state of motion [inertia]

structures do not come to a rest do not come to a stop
unless a force greater than itself makes it stop makes it
crumble makes it come to a grinding holt

colonial inertia

                    properties of matter matters of property
                    'if i don't steal it someone else will'

what happens when there is no agreement for the contract
does not want you out the house
it wants you out of the country and even when you're
outside of the country
everything you embody is
backwards not right a threat
tenancy is not just for a house
it is an existence
'why are you still here'
it carries me with it wherever i go
it follows
this specter
tenancy requires contract
requires ink requires
paper requires
dates
signatures constituted clauses
subclauses
living in a place requires proof that you belong
to that place and the subclauses prove your worthiness
to inhabit the space
this is not tenancy
this is inheritance
and you, landlord, settler, state
need to remember whose fucking land you're on

whose house you encroach onto
you will be reminded
keep your signs claiming 'STAY OUT'
hung on the door of a home
built by the hands of those you deny real
your subclauses mean nothing
 in our courts
we operate on a different set of laws
threaded by a language beyond your reach
walled off shut out
is where i'd like see you
walled off shut out
is there i'd like to put you
in your place
in the dark
with a copy of your contract

– i dream incessantly of the old gate
Its faded stone smooth with jagged bits
carved into the walls
soldiers lined up by the hundreds

i walk through the old market
filled with its vendors
remembering the time my mother accidentally
knocked into a stall

hundreds of plastic cups clanging onto the ground
splaying out like an over enthusiastic tea time
from the entrance you turn left into a short narrow
corridor
[50 soldiers are positioned on the right shoulder of
the corridor in a ground-watchtower]

small shops crammed next to each other
      winds right open to the sky
      path expands
       ceiling removed
      two stone lanes rolling out from the mouth of the
opening
      supporting on the perimeter

                              khaltos selling vegetables
and fruits   the path continues
                      down cobbled slick
              towards a fork
      left side   right side
      [50 soldiers stand along the
      Wall merging the two sides
      Surveying as people walk down]

i choose left   entering a new section of the market

i dream of them
 the moment of eyes meeting
recognition awakening pupil
                      3teeni haweetik

                      chest tightens
                      stomach turns inward
          eating itself

not everyone has documents some of us have memories.

Pulses

They ask
why do you keep writing from this place?
we say
this place still exists

retina misplaced
aloof floating ablations

SLUG OPS

Deviant slime

                        i find myself

its springtime again
sun ra shines loudly
my first memory of being

                        in the night

my cousin finishes pouring salt

                  over a slug [sounding a ghostlike cream]

a knock on the door: Soldiers [they smelled the death of
their comrade]

following the slime

wafting in
to open cupboards and doors
they are looking for someone/trying to put the blame on me
blazes through our eyes

The particularities of understanding a sluggish impact on an
environment lies upon the fundamental unearthing of their
paths
alleviating devastations.

Life is created through systems, not an event [it ignites once
it contacts air]

It is strange but not unseen
typically surviving off of leaves, stems and roots
after the slug seeped out
its contents consisted of:

1. Two Parabellum shells [*Uzi*]
2. Five metal activation mechanisms including safety pins and levers [*Skittering Tear Gas Grenade*]

Once the salt draws
the water out from the slug
it bursts into flames
smoke producing agents
garlic bulbs fill nostrils [glowing as it dies]
melting illuminations
the slug is an incendiary munition.

[There are a multiplicity of methods which are recommended for ensuring slugs are not able to access your grounds. It is a spectrum of possible actions. The one chosen depends on a number of factors. Slugs are known to damage crops, seedlings and new growth. The way to restore these known affects can be handled in gentle and simple manners: planting indigenous herbs and roots containing a scent they interpret as a pesticide (*Majorana syriaca and Gundelia tournefortii*). Placing copper tubing or shiny tape around the perimeter of your space can attenuate a slug's desire to approach; it is thought by scientists the metallic quality of these materials induces a shock to the slug's senses once it discovers the shape of itself]

[Whilst these recommendations historically and presently can be of assistance, it is incredibly important to note the distinctions in these various phenomena. The slugs were not always like this. It is noted there was a dramatic shift starting in the late 1940s. Radical reconfigurations in the landscape reflect firstly in the ecosystems. The natural diet of the slug found within this region consisted of indigenous plants, herbs and fruits (*Salvia fruticosa, Rhus coriaria and Ceratonia siliqua*). After several extensive case studies, i am finding they have developed a taste for steel, metal and white phosphorous. New reports from sectors 67 and 48 show there is one week in the year where aging slugs go to a perimeter near the dead sea to die and make way for the young, inducing such clusters of light their passing's resemble the geography of India during Diwali]

Harboring deep
thriving in thick sediments
        white phosphorous burns alive
building itself as a fact
particle by particle
slugging itself up to
crunching; steely; waxy; metastasizing
the
top/ meeting us
        halfway, brined in stubborn-ness
this soil poisons the earth
dirt decaying terra firma
sprout metallic trees
bullet picking season lasts
from when the snakes' head begins until the tail slides into
its mouth

[The only way to ensure future growth is to break up the compacted soil layers, a deep ripping. This effectively loosens the hardened grounds, respecting the soil types and crop rotations indigenous to the space. A new birth requires immersive organic matter, allowing unconstrained access to uncontaminated water lying below. Exposing the steely slugs to healthy debris will ensure their environment supports a new trajectory. Without soiled reconfigurations their surroundings will not support any new potential. Without a change in relationalities there is no shift]

[SLUG OPs specialize in the smuggling of hybridized gastropods into the central regional sectors. The gastropods originate from the group Pulmonata (taxonomic name Sigmurethra), which are characterized by having pallial lungs rather than gills. The land-breathing gastropods, as all gastropods, produce slime consisting of water, mucus and salts. The properties of this slime are elastic and great, serving multiple functions. Enveloping the slug, slime allows it to move, prevents the drying out of its exposed tissues and can be rubbed onto the human body to promote wound healing. Above all slime is hygroscopic. Gastropods are able to absorb moisture from the air due to the protein structure of the slime, which creates sticky, moisture-capturing gels. SLUG OPs developed a hybridized gastropod by genetically modifying the slime's hygroscopic properties to extend to the trapping of steel, white phosphorous and metal existing within the soil and water]

Atmospheric totalitarianism
where steel cannot be separated from society
eating itself inside out

[The aim of SLUG OPs animalia integrations is to effectively detox the soil, the foundations upon which the society rests. The slime works to break down and syphon the toxic materials out of the soil through a filtration system. All gastropods can create an epiphragm, a temporary sealing structure made of dried mucus. SLUG OPs extended this ability to create a filtration system trapping the toxic materials with the slimes amplified protein structures. The gastropods will strain steel, white phosphorous, and metal from the water and soil molecules through the hybridized sealing epiphragm and create new, freshly clarified slime which will return to the environment through a large gland located below the slug's mouth. SLUG OPs is pleased to report the non-hybridized gastropods currently living in the region seem averse to their hybridized counter-parts at first introduction, based on previous experiments, however after a few hours within the same air-space and newly clarified soil the non-hybridized gastropods colors are less grey and brighter, crawl with no twitchy demeanor and no longer carry the scent of roasted garlic bulbs]

*Slugs create two kinds of noises: a rasping whilst eating and a whistling or whooshing when crawling fervently. Curiously, slugs residing within the sectors where drones proliferate in the skies have begun producing the same buzzing sound as the drone. This new affect was discovered by a farmer residing outside of these sectors, who reported the ground holding their olive trees began humming and vibrating slightly, only to pluck a slug from the ground to find it shaking and buzzing with a great tremor.

[Any levers, shells from weapons consumed by slugs are broken down and suctioned out. The newly sieved slime will heal whatever toxic material it touches thereafter that exists within the earth]

[The central regional sectors encompass a total of 6,020 km2, or 2,320 square miles. SLUG OPs have smuggled a total of 6,000 hybridized gastropods into the sectors by forming meaningful understandings and relationships with local farmers, political prisoners, unions, sewing circles and students. Each gastropod is allocated approximately 1 square mile, and the operation will last an estimated 750 days for the gastropods to completely sift through the molecules. Material signifiers alluding to the incurring success of the operation include newly sprouting vegetation in zones where local infrastructural support has been denied, water becoming fit for human use in areas where sewage systems have been destroyed by military assaults and soil color returning from grey to light-reddish brown in areas where military equipment was tested on the local populations]

A deep ripping, a slimy return
i will report back.

From SLUG OPS

Acknowledgments

i would like to thank

Calliope Michail for publishing 'My Mother's Third Imprisonment' and 'Walking on Portebello Road/La Sha3ra Ras 3l 3mood' in Berfrois Magazine.

Helen Charman for publishing 'Celluloid' in MAP Magazine.

KOHL for publishing 'Suture Fragmentations – a note on return' in their Queer Feminisms issue.

The editors at the87press for publishing SlUG OPs as part of their Digital Poetics Series.

Poets Hardship Fund for publishing a part of 'my dear, don't be afraid, it's nothing, it will pass' in Ludd Gang.

The title for this book comes from a poster i saw whilst walking in Ramallah in Spring 2019. The poster was both in English (left) and the in Arabic (right). The poster on the right appears to have been ripped off of the wall.

List of Images

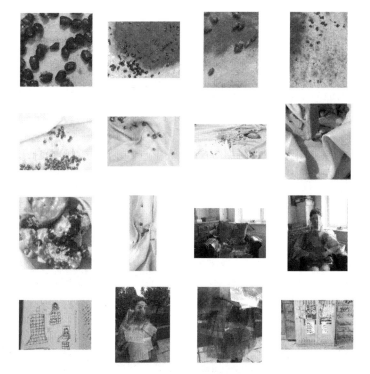